What Others Have Said...

This book is so NOT only for women.

First - Ms: de Vos does specifically look at her husband's grieving (Thank you) as well as the very real possibility of divorce. However, the book is written in the 1st person - from the Author's own perspective. It's her own story. Which makes it a really really valuable read for men too. If you (a man) are going through this process with your wife or partner, then you know a lot about the pain already. But because it may be so hard for her to talk to you (or for you to talk together) about her (and your) feelings and emotions (pain, anger, guilt, dispare, frustration, just being TIRED) this book could really help you gain perspective, and GO FORWARD - hopefully WITH her. You've been through a lot together, right? So where do you find your support? Your understanding? As the author says: "There are groups on social media that can be very supportive, yet they can also take you down a rabbit hole of self-pity." This is a good resource for you. The writing in this book is flowing and easy. The chapters (and clarity sessions) are short - bite sized bits that help you think and feel.

James Archer

This is a book where you will be taken in a journey of life's ups and downs. For every chapter there's a clarity session that provides hope and tips to move on with life.

A must read to those who are on the verge of giving up specifically to those who have been or trying to have children. You will face life with a different perspective after reading this book.

Elsa Mendoza

Through this honest account of her struggle with infertility, Rosemary offers companionship and hope to those who are experiencing the grief of lost dreams. She doesn't shy away from the hard stuff. Nor does she pretend that her longing for children can just be switched off. She pays tribute to her husband and recognizes his different ways of processing their experiences. Rosemary's training as an intuitive counsellor is evident in the 'Clarity Sessions' which follow each chapter and outline ways a person can connect with their own inner wisdom to find healing and joy.

Although clearly written for those whose dream to be parents is unfulfilled, Rosemary's first person account may help others to begin to appreciate, in part, the depth of grief experienced by those who do not choose to be child-free.

Lani East

I really enjoyed this book, even through the tough and sad parts. It's a poignant and intriguing ride through the author's experience. The chapter on handling rage was particularly interesting to me. It is so important to be able to feel and experience all the feelings associated with loss. I would definitely recommend this book to anyone dealing with loss; especially, the loss of infertility.

Mar Maldonado

MY LAST BFN

A Transformational Journey:

How To Create Joy After Infertility

Rosemary de Vos
INTUITIVE COUNSELLOR

Copyright © 2017 – Creating Flow

All rights reserved. No portion of this book may be reproduced, distributed or transmitted in any form or by any means, including photocopying, recording, or other electronic or mechanical methods, without the prior written permission of the publisher, except in the case of brief quotations embodied in critical reviews and certain other noncommercial uses permitted by copyright law.

Although the author and publisher have made every effort to ensure that the information in this book was correct at press time, the author and publisher do not assume and hereby disclaim any liability to any party for any loss, damage, or disruption caused by errors or omissions, whether such errors or omissions result from negligence, accident, or any other cause.

Neither the author nor the publisher assumes any responsibility or liability whatsoever on behalf of the consumer or reader of this material. Any perceived slight of any individual or organisation is purely unintentional.

Disclaimer

The book *My Last BFN, A Transformational Journey: How To Create Joy After Infertility* is a guide for women who are grieving from the lost that comes from of infertility.

It could also be a guide for those who are supporting a loved one who is struggling with giving up their dream of extending their family.

This book is written from two perspectives. A personal journey of a woman dealing with never having children and the Counsellor's perspective which provide the techniques used to overcome her grief which is in the form of Clarity Sessions.

The personal perspective does contain a few swear words as they contribute to the expression of emotions the author felt and it would be dishonest to edit them out.

This book does not replace professional counselling or health care as the information and resources in this book are for informational and educational purposes only.

Neither the author or the publisher can be held responsible for the information provided within this book.

Cover Photo: Stephanie Frey
Cover Design: Les Solot

Library and Archives Australia Cataloguing in Publication
de Vos, Rosemary, 1971 - , author

My Last BFN, *A Transformational Journey: How To Create Joy After Infertility*, 1st ed.
ISBN: 978-0-6481104-1-5

CONTENTS

Chapter 1 1

Negative Pregnancy Test 1

Chapter 2 7

Another Distraction 7

Chapter 3 13

Lessons In Life 13

Chapter 4 17

How Dare You 17

Chapter 5 23

Wedding Photos 23

Chapter 6 27

My Beautiful Embryo 27

Chapter 7 31

Support 31

Chapter 8 35

Physical Pain 35

Chapter 9 41

Christmas Tree 41

Chapter 10 45

Go Away World 45

Chapter 11 51

Food Glorious Food 51

Chapter 12 57

Different Choices 57

Chapter 13	63
Bah Humbug	63
Chapter 14	69
A Couple of Days	69
Chapter 15	75
Baby Clothes	75
Chapter 16	81
One Song	81
Chapter 17	85
I Wish	85
Chapter 18	89
My Life on Hold	89
Chapter 19	93
Radical Hysterectomy	93
Chapter 20	97
We Are Childless	97
Chapter 21	101
I'm Alone	101
Chapter 22	105
Waiting	105
Chapter 23	109
My Husband Is Grieving	109
Chapter 24	113
So They Say	113
Chapter 25	117

Exhaustion	117
Chapter 26	121
Keep On Trying	121
Chapter 27	127
Asking Questions	127
Chapter 28	131
Divorce	131
Chapter 29	135
But	135
Chapter 30	139
Heartbreaking	139
Chapter 31	143
A Pregnant Friend	143
Chapter 32	147
Opening to new possibilities	147
About The Author	149

Acknowledgements

I would like to thank Scott who has put up with all the tears, the insanity and allowed laughter to come into our lives.

Amanda Fox, Dorinda Povey, Sheridan Rowe and Yvette Merton who have been there for me as wonderful friends and confidantes over the years.

To my fur babies, Molly, Max, Coco and Banjo who would snuggle in with me at my lowest moments and offer me all their love.

To receive your free gift:
http://rosemarydevos.com/bfn-gift

Dedication

To all the women who would have been amazing mothers and who ARE amazing women.

"Healing is a matter of time, but it is sometimes also a matter of opportunity".

-Hippocrates.

Foreword

I work as an Intuitive Counsellor. I have a background in Mind Body Medicine, Holistic Counselling, Kinesiology and my skills continue to grow as I learn more every day.

I provide mentoring and counselling for clients as they go through the lows of life and I love every moment of it.

However, every time I create a new course for clients, I am forced to upgrade my life and walk my talk.

It's possible that this may happen for you as well without you even noticing it.

There may have been a time in your life when you have thought about doing something but you put it aside because it didn't fit into what was going on in your life. Something that you may not have been able to do if you had children.

I have found after working with many clients, that these seemingly random thoughts show up in ways that you would never have imagined.

I wonder if those random thoughts could now take you on an adventure where your life could be filled with joy, laughter and contribution?

I wonder if by not having children and becoming child free instead of childless, you could create your life beyond your imagination?

And I wonder, who you are as a strong, and influential woman with your undiscovered life in front of you...

I have written this book with the intention that you will know that you are not alone. You will know that you have a full life ahead of you, and that you will know that you are supported by your unborn baby spirits who will guide you every step of the way.

The book is structured so that you will read my personal experiences to assist you to connect with your feelings, and then the use Clarity Sessions to heal the grief, the anger and the fear we hold onto.

Your belief system may not align with the processes in the Clarity Sessions , yet what if you could humour me and maybe view them as fairy tales. Explore them from a space of wonderment and trust that you will receive whatever facilitation you require from reading this book.

If you feel that you need any extra support, please reach out to me to book a private consultation and we can work through this together.

Loving you... loving life...

Rosemary de Vos
Intuitive Counsellor
www.rosemarydevos.com

> Remember...
> If this book assisted you in any way,
> please let me know by leaving a review.

Introduction

I am a nulliparous female, which means that I have never given birth.

And if I became pregnant I would be classified as geriatric, which means that I am over 35 years old.

I have been through the lows and lows with the occasional optimistic high of trying to conceive a baby or two, and I am now done.

I started writing as a way for me to heal the deep, gut-wrenching pain I was feeling after I did a wee on a pregnancy test and it was negative, hence the name My Last BFN which stands for Big Fat Negative.

I've been a member of Trying To Conceive (TTC) groups and been a part of the desperation that women feel when their bodies don't give them what they want, and yet they are doing everything right.

We eat right, we don't drink alcohol (much), we exercise the right amount at the right time of our cycle, we take the right medication and the right supplements, we look at all forms of fertility treatment, and we time our sex lives so that we can have sex the right way and yet, we still are not pregnant.

This is my story and the processes I used to go through the grieving process of giving up the dream of having children.

After using the processes I describe in My Last BFN, I can now report that I no longer feel the need to have children in my life. I am happy, fulfilled and wake up each morning wondering what the day will bring.

I do have children in my life. I have nieces and nephews and cousins and friend's children who are wonderful beings growing up to be happy humans, and it is a joy to watch.

Going down the route of parenthood was not for my husband and me. It seems our life has other plans for us and it is certainly going to be an adventure, which I am excited about.

This is not a book about fertility options or fostering or adoption. We have looked at all avenues to creating a family, and none of them were for us, so if you were just about to write to me about some wonderful treatment or your experiences fostering or adopting, thank you for you thoughts, however, at this point in our lives, we have decided not to have children.

As you read this book, whether it's from beginning to end or you jump around, take the time to be gentle on yourself.

It took me four months to go through these processes, and I am now in the category of being child free instead of child less, as I am now in the place of choice rather than circumstance.

Just remember to breathe. It may take you longer for your life to transform, which is perfect. You have been through a huge amount of emotional upheaval, and it takes courage and strength to let it go.

You will know when you have finished grieving. You will know because life will start to fall into place again. All the struggle and heartache will be looked at as a sad story that happened to a version of you a while ago.

We are amazingly strong women, and as nulliparous females in this world, we have a lot to contribute.

Chapter 1
Negative Pregnancy Test

Lying in bed with tears streaming down my face, I'm wondering what on earth has happened to my life?

On the surface, it looks fairly normal. Or at least that's how I like to present it.

I have a loving husband, I have a business where I work as a counsellor, and my best friend just told me what an amazing impact I have had on my clients' lives over the years and yet...

I feel totally lost.

I'm falling into the space where the heartache is overwhelming.

Where the dreams of being a mother and having a family is completely and utterly gone.

I feel numb.

I feel angry.

I feel lost.

I feel lonely.

I feel sad.

I feel hurt.

And I am sobbing as I am writing this.

I can't stop sobbing, and truth be known, I don't want to.

My husband and I have spent the past 6 years and a lot of money trying to get pregnant, and 2 days ago the blood test for our frozen embryo transfer was negative.

A BIG FAT NEGATIVE!

I knew within myself that the blood results were going to be negative before I got the phone call. I knew I wasn't pregnant, just the same way you know the answer to a question before it has been asked. In fact, I started grieving a few days before the blood was taken to be tested because I felt the life force of the embryo move away from my body. All that was left was emptiness.

I can't believe how much time and energy I have spent on trying to conceive a baby. Even to the point where I wouldn't say "trying" because the word trying insinuates that you're actually never going to get to the pregnancy stage.

I have been wanting to be a mother long before I met my husband. And yet I was not completely comfortable with the idea. It's a weird feeling, wanting to have children, yet wanting a life without the responsibility of another and yet knowing that once a baby comes along, I would love it more than I could imagine.

I was stuck in a belief that you couldn't have it all. A family and a life outside of the family.

I grew up in a family where even though I was loved, my mother's career took precedence over everything. I didn't want my children to grow up in that environment, so it took me a very long time to do something of substance in my life and then when I got married my business slowed considerably while I focused on having children.

The same thing happened with getting married. I have never wanted to get married even though I liked the idea of getting married. I've even been engaged a couple of times, but going through with the wedding was something I struggled with. Yet now that I am married, I am extremely happy that I said: "I do."

Getting back to the BFN...

What makes a person go through six years of fertility treatments? Allopathic, herbal, homeopathic, alternative, spiritual and anything else we could think of? What makes a person build a business around a family that isn't here? What makes someone start again after grieving every cycle as her period comes and goes?

And when does it all stop?

For me, it stops today!

All the heartache, the emptiness and the craziness of hormone fluctuations stops right here, right now.

I am done with arranging my life around a baby that doesn't exist. I am done with putting my life on hold. I'm done with trying to manipulate my body and my husband's body into doing something that they simply don't want to do, especially as our infertility is unexplained.

I am done!

It's time for me to take my body back and to focus on my husband, my family, and friends, my business and clients and be grateful for what I have now and whatever shows up in the future.

That last sentence looks great on paper, yet all I want to do is stick my middle finger up at it.

I just want a baby. I don't care about the rest of the stuff. I don't care about anything else. Just a baby...

As I'm writing this, I'm feeling all the different emotions that come with grief and find myself slowly opening up to what I can do with the rest of my life.

I am currently 45 years old and know from personal experience and as a counsellor that I will need to keep feeling the depths of these emotions until I can love them completely for healing to occur. I've stopped crying for the moment and am wondering...

Who am I going to be and what am I going to do?

And the tears start flowing again...

Clarity Session

Feeling your emotions is one of the quickest ways to move through what you are going through, come out the other side and have clarity in your situation.

The whole idea of feeling something that is so painful may seem scary at first, yet if you really dive into the centre of your emotion, it will only take 90 seconds to 2 minutes to clear the level you are on.

When you are trapped by an emotion, it is hard to make decisions rationally, communicate effectively and love with compassion. Removing yourself from a situation where you are tempted to dump or vent all over a loved one is a kindness for them and for you.

This is one of the easiest techniques to feel your emotions and move on with your life.

Bring up the emotion so you are in it, so you can really feel it.

Remember, this emotion cannot kill you. You are stronger than you think.

Expand the emotion so that it feels 100 times larger than when you originally felt it.

Where can you feel the emotion? Is it inside or outside your body? Really connect with it.

Imagine you're diving into the emotion. Right into the core of it and then out the other side.

Keep diving through the emotion until you start to feel lighter.

Keep moving through until you feel a full release of the emotion.

You will know when you are done.

Sometimes emotions may feel a little sticky, and you may have trouble diving through them.

If this happens, ask your angelic guides to give you wings to help you fly through the emotion easily and gently.

They are happy to help.

Chapter 2
Another Distraction

Yesterday, the day after the Big Fat Negative pregnancy test, my husband took the day off work to be with me.

He is an amazing man, and I loved that he was making me a priority. However, instead of taking the time to feel what we were going through, we chose distraction and went bathroom and kitchen shopping.

We have been planning on renovating our home since we bought the house over a year ago. And as life goes, the renovations got delayed due to baby making (or lack thereof) and stresses over money.

I knew it would have been better for both of us to feel what was bubbling underneath the surface. All the hurt and pain of not being pregnant. The disappointment that there would never be little ones in our newly renovated house and the disconnect we were starting to feel as a couple. However, we couldn't miss this opportunity to get the renovation process started.

I do this a lot. We all do.

I distract myself with stuff to do. Websites and products to create. Things to watch on tv. Arguments to have, courses to study and space to fill.

In my professional capacity, I am very good at facilitating others to move through their feelings, yet we have all been taught from a young age to suppress our feelings.

I remember my grandmother telling me to stop crying at my other grandmother's funeral. Granted, I was being a little dramatic, yet it stopped me in my tracks, and the emotions came bubbling up years later.

We are all very busy and capable, yet instead of feeling and moving through our emotions, we distract ourselves with life, so we don't have to feel.

And even though no one is disappointed in me as such, they may be disappointed we don't have children, but they are not disappointed in me, and I've learned to keep myself distracted so that I don't feel whatever is bubbling under the surface.

I'm well aware that I am doing it, so I've asked my other than conscious mind for help.

Asking it to help me feel. Feel the pain, the hurt, the emptiness so that it doesn't appear in other areas of my life.

The emotions are just too strong, too raw to feel. If I feel them, I could possibly die from the pain. So they spread. They spread into my body, my relationships and other areas of my life. I am disconnecting from my life, yet from the outside, it would seem that all is well in my world.

I just caught myself looking up a new business name as I want to end my business partnership with my husband.

A distraction, yes, but so much more than that.

It's a way for me to feel free again. Free from the pain of being in a relationship with a man who I can't have children with.

It's a way for me to disconnect from my feelings and pretend that life will be great if I have something else to focus on.

It's a way for me to fool myself so that I don't ever have to feel like I am dying inside.

Energetically it feels great for me to have my own business, so at this point, the distraction continues.

I would have been a wonderful mum. We would have been amazing parents with so much love to give. I'm not saying we would have been perfect, we would have done our best to be there for the small humans as they grow into larger ones.

My husband had his helicopter ready (he's the worry wort), and I was ready with an open heart to see whatever was required at that moment in time. We were ready for the laughter and the tears, the cheekiness, and the joy. We were even ready for any heartache, knowing full well that you're never really ready for the heartache until it occurs.

And now where is all that love supposed to go?

Who am I supposed to love now?

All the fun, all the giggles, all the wonder and the dreams. What am I supposed to do with them now?

Nothing... absolutely nothing.

The dream of having our family is gone. I am not a mother, my husband is not a dad, and we won't have that bond that I see among my friends who have children.

We will have to create something different.

As I'm writing this, I can feel all the expectations, the dreams, the fantasy of what my life would have been with our imaginary family falling away. Leaving me open, heartbroken, shattered to my core, knowing that the grief, the loss and the struggle of infertility is opening me up to something new. I know it will.

As I allow the distractions come and go, I just don't know when my life will start again.

And the tears continue to flow...

Clarity Session

Distractions take you away from feeling, which can be good and not so good depending on what's happening in your world at the time.

If you are feeling emotions bubbling below the surface, it may be a good idea to go through Clarity Session – 1 and dive into your emotions.

However, if you don't have the time or space to do so, a distraction which will allow you to see that there is a whole world of joy available for you is a wonderful thing.

By looking beyond your issue and making life bigger than you is a way to give you the energy and motivation to create something out of your pain.

Most distractions are ones that are simply delaying the timing where you will be forced to feel what you are going through and it's best to acknowledge it as such.

When you are able to acknowledge what you are doing, you can also make an appointment with your feelings to create a time and space to connect with them and heal what you are going through.

In the meantime, asking some questions to your other than conscious mind will allow it to get on board with what you are going through, as it is the part of your being that runs the show.

Its language is one of the questions, however, when you ask a question, don't go looking for an answer, simply let it go, and you'll find the answers show up in ways that you would never have expected.

Some sample questions are:

"Who am I today?"

"What can I do today that would bring more joy into my life?"

"What lessons are being shown to me?"

"What if this feeling could be healed easily and gently?"

"What if I could see a miracle today?"

The more you ask of your other than conscious mind, the more you will be opened up to your wondrous life.

Chapter 3
Lessons In Life

I was talking to my friend who is a meditation teacher, and she suggested that I meditate on what is the lesson for not being able to have children.

My first reaction, even though I know it's a good idea is, "Oh Joy! If I'm being tested for something, then the Universe can go f* itself!" Not the most spiritual of reactions, but a very human one.

At the moment, even with my knowledge as a Counsellor, I don't really care about lessons or what I am going to gain from this experience, I just want to have a family!

I don't care about a Universe that won't give me things I can't handle, I want a baby!

I don't care about who I can help with my experiences, I want to be a Mum!

I don't care whether what I'm writing is going to be for any reason other than my own blabberings, I am in pain and life sucks!

So, Universe, If you're listening and this is some sort of test, you can go f* yourself!!!!

Maybe I'll get to the meditation another time.

As I continue to sob

Clarity Session

Many believe that we are on this planet to learn from lessons. That we are in a school of sorts and we need to learn and grow while we are here.

Others believe that we are simply on the planet to experience what we are unable to experience anywhere else.

Whatever the belief system, by connecting with your inner knowing, you are able to find out your reasoning behind what is going on in your life.

The first step is learning how to connect with your knowing.

It is easy, yet it may take a little practice.

1. Take a deep breath and relax.

2. Ask yourself where you are – inside your body, outside your body or somewhere else?

3. If possible, ask yourself to come into your body and fill it up so that it overflows through your skin. Your body is now inside your being.

4. Ask your body to show you a yes.

5. Ask your body to show you a no.

6. You'll receive a response, and it could be different every time you ask yourself these questions, but trust that your body is honestly communicating with you.

7. Some questions to ask are:

"Did I choose (your issue) before coming to this planet?"

"Is this situation a lesson I need to learn from?"

"Is this a lesson I have experienced many times?"

"Is it possible for my other than conscious mind to complete the lesson on my behalf?"

"Will my other than conscious mind please complete this (your issue) on my behalf now?"

"Is this an ancestral issue?"

"Is this a past life lesson?"

Keep asking questions, and you'll find that you will receive clarity from your inner knowing. Trust that it is there to support you through your grieving process and that you are not alone.

Chapter 4
How Dare You

F* YOU!!!!!

How dare you give me the thought, the inclination, the opportunity to get pregnant and go through fertility treatment after fertility treatment yet knowing that this is all for nothing!

Nothing!

No pregnancy.

No birth.

No baby.

No toddler,

No child.

No teenager.

No beautiful human to come into this world and contribute their gifts with the rest of humanity.

How dare you!

What is the point of having a thought if it's not going to eventuate into the physical embodiment?

I get that we have many thousands of thoughts throughout the day, and I get that most of those thoughts aren't even mine to do anything with. And I get that some thoughts would not be great if they actualised but the ones that we would like, the ones that would give me joy and open my heart to love, why wouldn't those come into our reality?

Why wouldn't they be the gift that could transform my life into something spectacular?

I hear about the power of positive thinking all the time, but really it's a crock! Things happen whether they are positive or negative. Things just happen, and most of the time I have absolutely no control over it... Yes, yes, I only have control over how I react to it... I've heard it all before.

So what's the deal? Do I have any control over what happens in my life?

What is the point of having hopes and dreams when they come smashing down around me?

I call bullshit on life.

I get up in the morning, I contribute to people around me, I have intentions that certain things will happen in my life and sometimes they will and sometimes they won't.

Who knows?

Who's holding the puppet strings anyway?

This power that is more than happy to be in control, more than happy to manipulate and control my every desire, my hopes and my dreams.

Certainly not me. My life is definitely not how I planned it to be.

Ok, then, how about I get out of bed every morning, and the puppet master can tell me how to live my life in every moment. No plans, no expectations, no thinking ahead, no thinking at all!

My life has nothing to do with me.

No tears at the moment... let's give rage a try!!!!!!

Clarity Session

Rage is a healthy way to move through our emotions and the grieving process.

Yelling into your pillow, screaming at the trees in nature, writing it down and spewing words across the page all allow the rage to leave our body.

Allowing the rage to infect others is not so healthy, so if you can do this process on your own, it will help you and be kind to your friends and family.

This technique allows us to transform rage into an intensity that can assist us in being the catalyst for transformation.

1. Get prepared. Be in nature, alone with a pillow or have a place for writing available.

2. Ask your other than conscious mind to assist in the release and transformation of the rage in your body and your morphic field.

3. Let it out! Scream, Yell, Write, Cry and Feel It To Your Core!

4. Do not harm yourself physically in any way. This is a healing process, and by giving it to your pillow, the trees, and the paper/computer, you are allowing it to transform into an energy you can use for transformation.

5. Keep going until you feel empty. Many of you may start giggling or feel lighter.

6. You can do this process as many times as you require.

The interesting thing about rage or anger is that it is an emotion that can give us motivation. It can give us the power to stop injustice in a moment, and it can be used with love.

When you allow yourself to feel the rage and give it over to your pillow, nature or your writing, we also have the ability to call it up at any time you choose.

At any time you are in an unsafe environment bring up the intensity of that rage. Not to attack anyone, but to repel anyone who may be attracted to fear.

At any time you are called to step in to prevent an injustice, bring up the intensity of rage. Once again, not to attack, yet the intense energy will transform the situation.

This is the step beyond rage to transform into love.

Chapter 5
Wedding Photos

I just got up to get something to eat and walked past our wedding photos.

The two of us looking at each other, connected to each other for the rest of this life. Looking forward to creating a family and new adventures together.

And yes, we have been on many adventures and will probably go on many more, yet it will just be the two of us.

My husband and I had a funny wedding. He and I didn't "fall in love" in the traditional sense of the word. We knew that we loved each other, and we were going to be together, but we felt the "in love" stage come after we got married. It was almost as if our marriage was arranged by the universe. (Small u because I am still angry and it doesn't deserve it!).

We were set up by a mutual colleague/friend, we made decisions when we dated by words falling out of our mouths before we even knew we were saying them. It was a lot of coincidences and synchronicities that allowed us to come together as a couple.

So here we are 6 years later ready to close our business and figure out what to do with our life as a childless couple.

What do childless couples do?

I don't mean couples who have consciously chosen not to have children, but the ones who desperately wanted to expand their family and are left with a gaping hole in their lives. Do they join clubs? Try new experiences? Meet new people who are also childless and don't have to worry about babysitters or times to pick up their kids from school?

What am I going to do with all the time and energy that I've put into researching fertility treatments?

Who would have thought, looking at my wedding photos that the woman who was gazing lovingly into the eyes of her new husband would waste so much time on forums and Facebook groups supporting and being supported by other women who are researching and obsessing and feeling this uncontrollable need to have children?

No one... not by looking at those photos.

And now it's just the two of us.

Not the two of us with the potential of more.

Not the two of us creating a family together.

Just the two of us.

Isn't that supposed to happen after the kids have grown up and moved out? Isn't it supposed to be when we become empty nesters?

Nope, it's happening now, 20 or so years too early.

It's just the two of us.

I feel like it's us against the world, which I know isn't true because we have amazingly supportive friends and family and yet...

It's just the two of us, and sometimes it's just me.

I think it's time for a cry...

Clarity Session

Your life is bigger than just you.

When you are stuck in the "Woe is me!" pity party, life is small and painful.

Yet there will come a time when you are ready to step out and contribute to your life by contributing to the lives of others.

Contributing can come in many forms.

1. Calling a friend to ask them how they are without talking about yourself.

2. Saying hi to a neighbour.

3. Smiling to a cashier.

4. Sending love to a telemarketer even though you are still saying no.

5. Volunteering in your community.

6. Talking/giving love to plants.

By saying you are ready to contribute to life, it doesn't mean that you have to go big or even do anything at all. When you are actually ready, little things will start to show up in your life, and you'll automatically open up to a life that is full of love and abundance.

You can even ask your spirit baby to help you with this as many unborn spirits become guides as they wait until it is time for them to be born.

Chapter 6
My Beautiful Embryo

I FEEL WEIRD BECAUSE I KNOW that I am not pregnant, yet I had a beautiful little embryo placed inside my uterus. When the transfer occurred, there was life force attached to the embryo, and now there is nothing.

Where did the life force go?

What's the embryo doing?

What were the reasons why the embryo didn't embed itself and snuggle into the walls of my uterus to grow into a beautiful, healthy baby (or two)?

Intellectually I know the answers to these questions, but emotionally, that's another thing altogether.

Why did the life force or spirit change its mind? It had the potential of becoming a baby and yet chose not to. I wish it would talk to me and tell me what's really going on. Not just the physical, intellectual information but the emotional and spiritual reasoning behind not taking the chance to become a human being.

Did it not like the timing?

Maybe it didn't want to be a Leo, maybe it would have preferred to be another star sign.

Maybe it doesn't want me as a mum or my husband as a dad... ouch.

Maybe it doesn't like our house or our furbabies.

Maybe it didn't like the life path that was planned for that little embryo.

Who really knows? Not me, that's for sure.

All I know is that there was once the potential of a baby or two and now there is nothing but cells ready to be expelled over the next few days.

I would love to be able to connect with the spirit that would have been my baby. I thought I had over the past few months. I'd been doing the exercises from Walter Malkein's book *Spirit Babies* and felt two very distinct energies around me, ready to embody the physical.

I have felt them in different ways over the past 6 years, but more so when we started down the IVF route. I felt them up until two days before my last BFN, and then they were gone without an explanation.

And now I have an embryo without any life force.

The two week wait (2WW) is an anxious time waiting, wondering if you are pregnant, yet this is worse. The grieving of the potential of a baby is... well it feels like someone has died. I would imagine that waiting for a miscarriage would be even worse than this and then yes there is worse than that. And at the moment I am grieving for it all.

All the potential that did not occur. All the pain, the anger, the heartache, the sorrow.

Once there was something and now, nothing...

Clarity Session

Connecting with spirit babies can be very healing as they are in your life for a reason. Even though they may not join you in the physical world for various reasons, they are in your spiritual world, and many become their future mother's guides.

Doing this process on a regular basis will build the connection between you both.

Take a few deep breaths and connect with your heart space.

Ask your Other Than Conscious Mind, your Angels, the Divine to assist you with communicating with your spirit babies.

Ask any question you wish to your spirit baby.

Trust that the answers will come to you at the appropriate time.

Imagine a huge bubble of love surrounding your spirit baby.

Imagine a huge bubble of love surrounding you.

Imagine both bubbles integrating and becoming one.

Go about your day, knowing that you are connected with your spirit baby.

If you find that emotions come up such as anger and hurt, please use Clarity Session 1 to resolve them. You can even do this on your spirit baby's behalf, knowing that you are open and ready to love it completely, as there are times when your spirit baby feels lost and lonely, and it may need a little assistance to connect with you completely.

Chapter 7
Support

It has taken me six years to open up to my friends and family about the struggle that we have had creating our family. It is still difficult for me to talk about it.

I said to my dad two days after my period started, "I've had a bit of a cry and now I'm over it!"

What a load of bullshit!

I have a friend who I've known since childhood who called me the other day. It's one of those friendships where you just pick up where you left off no matter how long it's been. She had been through fertility issues and now has a lovely son. She gets it. She gets the struggle, the heartache, the pain and while we were chatting on the phone, she cried with me.

We cried together, and I felt so supported.

Yes, you can have empathy for another, yet unless you have been through the same process as someone else, you really don't get it. You can understand the concept, but you don't get it.

I didn't get it when she was hurting, how could I?

I had never experienced what she was feeling. Never felt the loss of not seeing the potential of the child come into reality. Never felt the grief, the hurt and the anger that comes with losing the dream of a family.

I'd only conceptualised it and thought I understood.

Even if you have gone through the same experience as another, there will still be differences because I will be experiencing it through my filters, my ideas, and my understanding and you'll be experiencing it through yours.

And yet we cried together.

When another person is crying with me, usually I start to feel responsible for them, and I stop crying to look after them. Not this time. I didn't have the energy to feel responsible for anyone. The pain is raw.

This last cycle was the cycle we told people about. We told my parents, my husband's family and some of our friends. The ones we knew were going to be supportive.

I love that we were finally able to open ourselves up to the support that was required as we completed our last cycle. I loved that our friends and family were able to support us to the best of their ability.

Even though I feel very alone going through this process, I know that any one of them will be there for us which is so much easier than going it alone.

Thank you to my beautiful friend who cried with me. I have a feeling it won't be the last time.

And now I can breathe for a moment...

Clarity Session

Support is so important when you are grieving for the loss of your family.

A dream of having babies and a loving family is something that we are missing out on in this moment and letting go of that dream can be one of the hardest things to do.

Yes, you are supported by the energetic and angelic realm, however, having someone to talk to in the physical world can be really helpful.

Partners can be very helpful, yet they are going through their own grieving process.

There are groups on social media that can be very supportive, yet they can also take you down a rabbit hole of self-pity.

A counsellor, a friend who understands or even a helpline can bring you a world of relief simply to know that you are listened to and loved.

It took me six years to open up to another about the pain I was feeling, so give yourself a break if you feel alone even if you have spoken to someone.

Let your other than conscious mind know that you are ready for someone to come into your life to simply listen and cry with you for 15 or so minutes so you can be loved and you never know who will show up in your life.

Chapter 8
Physical Pain

For the last two days, I have been in pain. Physical pain.

My period has arrived, and I feel like I am losing my insides.

It's not as heavy as it usually is, but the pain is worse than it ever has been and as much as I hate the pain, it's better than feeling the grief of never having children.

Sharp pain, stabbing pain, angry pain. Purging my body of what was never to have been.

Distracting pain so that hopefully, I will start to feel numb to the grief.

At least I'm not crying. I think I am over that part...

I just want this to be over. I want the grief to be gone, the possibilities to be gone and all the stories of other people's pregnancies to be gone.

When I'm feeling the physical pain, I'm thinking that it is like having contractions and I'm using the visualisations and breathing techniques to ease the pain. And guess what? They work!

I could have used them during childbirth, if only I had been given the chance.

Of course, I know they work, I've used them with clients who are in pain, yet I've never used them on myself, so I only have second-hand experience of them.

I really am a very skeptical person. Even though I intellectually know something works, I don't actually believe that it will work for me, until it does. I think many people are like that and so they should be. Don't take other people's word for it, find out yourself if you ever need to.

That doesn't mean that I disbelieve what other people's experiences are. If it is true for someone, it is true for them. They don't need my validation.

You may have noticed that I am in my head at the moment. The pain from my period passed a couple of days ago, and I'm not in the mood to feel the tears that are threatening to flow if given the go ahead.

I couldn't write while I was in physical pain. I was concentrating on getting through it. Getting out the other side. I couldn't run away from it like I can emotional pain. I was forced to deal with it.

I know that if I don't look at the emotional pain of never having children, it will be forced upon me as well.

The pain will find a way to manifest in a way that I will not be able to run from... it may be relationship issues, a disease of some sort, financial issues or something else that I have no idea of at this point in time...

So I am asking the Universe for help.

"Universe will you please help me resolve the underlying grief, anger, and fear that is keeping me stuck in these emotions? Will you please help me resolve any desires I have to feel physical pain rather than the emotional pain that is required for me to be free and enjoy life again? Will you please open me up to a new dream for my life and allow the old dream to ease out of my life?"

I now have an inkling of an understanding of why people cut themselves.

Tomorrow, I will feel some emotions again...

Clarity Session

There is always an emotional source behind the physical pain.

It doesn't matter what sort of pain it is or how it occurred, if you ask your body, you will find that it is connected to your mother, your father or a memory of something that has occurred in your life that hasn't been resolved.

This technique has been used on many of my clients over the years to ease and let go of the physical pain.

1. Connect with the pain in your body.

2. Ask the pain some questions:

    "How old are you?"

    "What size are you?"

    "What do you taste like?"

    "What do you smell like?"

    "If I touched you, how would you feel?"

    "What do you sound like?"

    "What emotion or memory is attached to you?"

3. Imagine the pain enveloped in a bubble of unconditional love.

4. Bring the pain outside of your body into a healing space in front of you.

5. Ask it to untangle from you.

6. Imagine it is being healed as the bubble of unconditional love moves around it and infuses through it.

7. Bring the healed bubble of unconditional love into your heart space, knowing that this memory and anything else holding it in place has been completed.

If you can't connect with a memory, ask your other than conscious mind to help out to see if there are any feelings that are being suppressed at the moment and if it can resolve them on your behalf.

Chapter 9
Christmas Tree

Yesterday, still in bed after 2 days of excruciating period pain, my body was feeling weak, and I was ensconced in a murder mystery book. I haven't given myself the pleasure of reading for such a long time. It has been a choice between work and getting pregnant. These have been my 2 options.

My husband, who loves Christmas decided that it was the day to put the Christmas Tree up. Usually, he would want to get it up mid-November, so the11th of December was late for him.

I'm not a huge fan of Christmas. Historically, Christmas created a lot of stress and expectations in my primary family, so I have tended to avoid it. This is my perspective as other members of my family love Christmas.

It has been fun over the years putting up the tree with my husband. He puts on the cheesy Christmas songs and the animals try and run away with tinsel or baubles. He then gives the cats a talking to so they won't climb the tree which makes no difference.

But yesterday, I didn't go and help. I was reading. When dinner was ready, I got up to have a look at the fantastic job he had done. He really is very good at decorating trees.

And I started to cry.

Now I know why as an adult I don't really like Christmas. I'm not a religious person, and although I believe that there was a spiritual master named Jesus, I don't necessarily buy into celebrating his birthday. If that was the case, I wouldn't be buying presents for everyone, I would be enjoying people's company with an open heart knowing that Jesus has our back. That is my preference.

And everyone who has gift giving as their top love language would probably disagree with me.

I don't like it because I don't have a family to share it with. I don't have children to play with. I don't have the enjoyment of sharing wisdom with them and opening them to the possibility of a spiritual day rather than something that is commercially based.

I know I've contradicted myself, but at this moment, I really don't know what I'm talking about.

All I know is that I saw the Christmas tree, beautiful and shiny and I started to cry. No, I started to weep.

My wonderful husband simply held me as I let it all out.

The stupid tree is now in our dining room reminding me to feel my emotions for the next month or so. I can't even close the door to the dining room because it is the room in the middle of our house!

This is what I was saying before... if you resist something, it will show up somewhere else. Somewhere unexpected and every day you'll have to walk past it, and it will remind you to feel.

Well, I'm feeling something now, and I'm ready to rip it from its perch and throw it from one end of the house to the other!!!

Clarity Session

Have you ever heard of the saying, "What you resist persists and grows stronger"?

Well, unfortunately, this is true. When you energetically push against something that you don't want, you are giving it the energy to get stronger and push back.

Life is about flow and ease, and when you resist, a barrier is formed in the shape of what you are resisting, and there is no getting away from it.

You can never get away from what you are meant to feel. It is simply not possible because if you don't feel it in the present moment, you will be reminded of it in another.

The trick is to feel what you are feeling in this moment. Right here, right now. Move through it, as in Clarity Session – 1 and go on to the next moment in your life.

If it is an inappropriate time to feel, make an appointment with the Divine to feel.

If after you have used the technique to feel, it is still hanging around, you might find that the feeling actually belongs to someone else and you are picking up on it.

An easy way to resolve this is to ask the feeling to be returned to sender and go on with your day.

It's time to take your power back from everything you have ever resisted in your life. This doesn't mean that these things are going to happen. It simply means that you have more energy to stay in the flow of life.

1. Take a deep breath and relax.
2. Ask, "Please bring all energy back to me that is holding any resistance in place."

Whenever you feel resistance in your life, know that it is simply an emotion, just like any other that you can feel, move through and come out the other side with clarity.

Chapter 10
Go Away World

The day I went shopping for a new bathroom and kitchen is backfiring on me.

After 4 days of being in bed, the builders are ready to measure and quote on our new kitchen and bathrooms. But I don't want to get out of bed. I'm not ready. I don't want to.

But I have to.

Because I work for myself, I've done a bit of work here and there but mostly nothing. And that amount of nothing can be done from bed which can also be used as a distraction when I don't want to feel anything.

But having someone come into my house means that I have to get up, shower and act like a semi-decent human being. This is a tough call when my dreams of having a family have been shattered into a million pieces and have cut me in the process.

I know I'm being very dramatic!

The first builder is coming this afternoon sometime. The next is tomorrow and the next one the day after.

One of my friends is taking me out for a pedicure tomorrow, and I'm getting my hair done the day after.

Then maybe I can go back to bed.

I can see how easily grief can turn into depression. All the signs are there, and if I give into it, that would be the last you would see of me for a while.

I know that if I felt these emotions, the process would go a lot quicker and it would be unlikely to turn into depression, yet knowing is a lot easier than doing.

I feel like if I felt them all, I would die. I know that is not true.

I feel like if I felt them all, my head would explode. I know that is not true.

I feel like if I felt them all, I would drown into the abyss of grief and never be happy again. I know that this is not true.

I know this because I have seen others feel their feelings and open up into a new possibility of living.

I know this because I've seen little kids do it easily and effortlessly.

I know this because I've done it myself, but for some reason, I feel the need to punish myself and hold these emotions close so that I will continually feel the pain of not having children ever again.

I'm resisting going through the process.

The writing is helping the emotions come to the surface, but it is also hindering the fact that I don't want to lose my train of thought by completing the process and moving through the emotions completely.

Who am I writing this for?

Me or the millions of other women who will never have children?

At this point, it's a bit of both.

I'm changing it so that it's for me. Any other reason to write about this is simply a distraction so that I won't feel what I need to feel.

And at the moment I'm feeling hatred, and I'm not ready to be forced into the world.

Clarity Session

Staying present is the way to happiness.

When you are in the moment of now, this is all that is. It is the space of flow, of love, of peace and of joy.

But how do you get present when you are constantly thinking of what to do next, and you are making choices from your experiences of the past.

Every time you feel unhappy, unwell or overwhelmed simply do this technique to get you back into the moment of now.

1. Take a deep breath and relax.

2. Ask yourself some questions:

    "Where am I?"

    "Am I inside?"

    "Am I outside?"

    "Am I cold or am I warm?"

    "What am I wearing?"

    "Am I hungry or am I thirsty?"

By asking these questions, you will be able to bring yourself into the present moment and out of your cognitive or monkey mind, which is distracting you from feeling.

The present moment is the moment where you are able to breathe, relax and be more productive than you ever thought possible.

The present moment is where creativity, healing, motivation and happiness reside. And the more you practice being present that easier the grieving process will be.

Chapter 11
Food Glorious Food

There is not enough food in this world to fill the hole in me.

I have never been an emotional eater. In fact, my usual tactic when I am stressed is to stop eating, but things seemed to have changed. Now all I want to do is eat.

The other day I asked my husband to bring me home some danish. He bought me three, thinking that they could last a little while, yet knowing that they would be gone very quickly. The first was delicious. Just what I needed.

The second danish was when I knew that my psyche had changed. As I was taking a bite, I thought to the danish, "I hate you!" I have never felt like that about food before. I've never felt like that about anything before. I've always loved food. The nourishment, the wholesomeness, the energy and the enjoyment it has given me. Never before have I looked at food, hated it and then eaten the hate. And I was conscious that I was doing it!

Last night, I had about 5 mouthfuls of food left on my plate. I was full, yet still, I ate those last mouthfuls. I stuffed it in my mouth and was so full I felt sick. I was punishing myself, and I was hating myself. I woke up this morning still full and still feeling sick.

Punishing myself and hating myself.

Punishing myself and hating myself.

Punishing myself and hating myself

For no particular reason except for the fact that the hate that has been stored somewhere deep inside me is coming up to say, "I HATE YOU!"

I hate you for the life that you have.

I hate you for being you.

I hate you for the choices you have made.

I hate you, and I'm projecting it onto the food that used to be so nurturing to me.

What do I do with this information? How do I release this hate and allow myself to stop the self-punishment?

I know intellectually this is not true, however, in the primal depths where this hate lives it needs to come out, be seen, be heard.

This hate, this rage, this pure unadulterated lava flowing out of me needs to be loved.

Not the love that makes me enjoy this, but the sort of love I would give to a little one who was in so much pain that it breaks your heart to bear witness.

As the tears flow, I say...

"Beautiful body, it's not your fault. It's not your fault that you are unable to have children. I am so sorry that I have made you feel that this is your burden to carry. It is no one's fault. If you look into the energy of it, you will see that this is a choice that I made before I came to earth so that I would be able to feel everything that I am feeling. That I would be able to do everything that I am doing and to be able to love you, body, more than you could ever know."

"Beautiful body, are you willing to let go of the hurt, the pain, the anger, the fear and the grief that not being able to fall pregnant is allowing you to feel?"

"Beautiful body, are you willing to open yourself to the possibility that you are allowed to be fit, healthy and happy even if you are never able to fall pregnant?

"Beautiful body, are you willing to accept my apology for making you feel like this is all your fault when it clearly is not. It is an experience I chose that you were willing to play out for me and for that I am eternally grateful."

What if you could let it all go...

Would you?

Could you?

When? Now?

My body is beautiful, and it is loving and giving, and without it, I would be a ball of energy floating around not being able to have all the experiences of life here on earth. So, body, I thank you and release you from any wrong doing you may have taken on.

Well, that feels a lot lighter.

When I imagine myself eating I don't feel hatred anymore. In fact, I almost feel like laughing.

But not quite... still some more work to be done...

Clarity Session

Emotional eating is a way to repress and suppress what we are avoiding feeling. It also gives us an opportunity to feel without processing the feeling, so we are stuck with the energy in our cellular memories as we eat the food.

Connecting and communicating with your body as though it is a small child can be therapeutic.

Nurturing and loving your body, even though it is not doing as you would like, is the first step to releasing the judgement and resentment you have towards it and the grief you are feeling.

By using this technique, you will find that you will have more compassion towards what you have put your body through during the journey of infertility.

1. Take a breath and relax.
2. What would you say to someone that has been beaten up and bruised both emotionally and physically?
3. How would you take care of someone that needs to be nurtured and loved?
4. Look into a mirror – into your left eye.
5. Tell yourself, as though looking after a small, hurt child that you will love it no matter what.
6. Tell your body that it no longer has to carry the burden of infertility.
7. Tell your body that you will love it and that nothing and no one will ever hurt it again.

8. Have a conversation with your body as though it is a small child and let it know that you will love it and protect it from now on.

Remember, you are the adult, and you will care and love your body because, even though it may not feel like it, your body has been there for you every step of the way.

Even though you have judged it and resented it in the past, it's time for you to heal and move into the next stage of your relationship with your body.

It's time for love, compassion and a lot of tender loving care for your bruised and beaten up body.

Chapter 12
Different Choices

There is a parallel universe where I have children. I know it. It feels so close and yet it is not my life. In fact, there are probably a couple of them.

There's one where I have one child.

There's another where I have 2.

And another where I have 3.

And with one of them, there is a different husband. It's really weird.

I met my husband when I was 37, and he was 39, and before then I had dated quite a few men and had been engaged to be married twice before. And if I had made different choices over the years, those parallel universes may have been my reality.

It's unlikely that I would still have been married if I had gone through with the weddings, but I have a feeling that I would have had children.

Or I could have chosen not to be with my husband and ended up with someone else!

So what's better? Happily married without children or unhappily married with children.

Neither are better, neither are worse. They simply are.

Sometimes, when I'm in between the awake and asleep states I can almost jump into the other realities, and I would know the experience of having little kids jumping all over me in the morning. Or not having enough sleep at night because I'm up looking after a baby. It's so close I can touch it, and yet it's not in my reality.

I don't understand why I've been given the urge, the want, the need to have children if I was never going to have them. Maybe I just made wrong choices.

We all come to crossroads in our life and given the same choice we would choose differently depending on where we are in our journey. So, what if I had taken the other road?

What would my life be like now?

My preference would be to be with the husband that I have now, as I would choose him over and over again and to have 2 gorgeous kids.

I would have loved to have met my husband years before I did so that I wouldn't be 45 and grieving over a lost dream. I would have preferred to be a younger mum. I would have preferred, I would have preferred.

But I didn't choose differently, and apart from the lack of children in our home, my life is pretty bloody good.

I have so much love flowing to me from friends, family and our 4 animals, I just have this gaping hole that makes me wonder what my life would be like if I had taken another path.

It's time to send love and goodbyes to the other me in the other universes and come back to this reality. I understand that life is not necessarily greener and I'm sure she has a wonderful life with her ups and downs. I'm sure she has her heartaches and her joy, and I'm sure she wonders "What if?" occasionally.

However, one thing I have learned is that I never know what life has in store for me. I have my preferences, yet the journey I am on will show up in ways that I could never have imagined.

And now I wonder what's coming next...

Clarity Session

Are you the leader in your life?

Maybe yes, maybe no!

Many who go through the infertility journey give their power over to the process. The power goes to the fertility specialists, and we get lost as we disconnect from who we are.

As we disconnect with the infertility journey, it is time for us to be the leader in our life.

This process allows you to centre yourself in your power and be the leader in your life, your ancestral line and bring your energy back from other aspects of you throughout the Multiverse.

1. Take a deep breath and relax.

2. Ask yourself some questions:

    "Am I the leader in this life?"

    "What if I was the leader in this life?"

    "Who would I be?"

    "What would I feel?"

    "How would I behave?"

    "What would I be doing?"

By asking these questions and not requiring an answer from your cognitive mind, you are asking your energy that is scattered and being pulled away from you to come back to you, perfect, whole and complete. Full of love, full of light, infused with the highest expression of who you really are.

When you do this process, you will be strengthening your core, your inner strength which will assist with your healing.

Chapter 13
Bah Humbug

My mum rang me today to talk to me about Christmas day. I told her, I didn't really want to go. There will be kids there, and extended family and I'll have to put on a brave face when all I want to do is cry. I really don't want to go.

Her response... you'll have to get over it. It's in the past now.

Well, you know what? It doesn't feel like it's in the past to me. It feels like the present. It feels like right now. It feels excruciating!

Granted, not as excruciating as last week, but it's still painful.

It's about 2 weeks until Christmas day and the thought of going brings tears to my eyes. I can tell that it's going to be horrible. I can tell that I'm going to be holding back the tears. I can tell all these things and yet I could be surprised.

2 weeks is a long time to process this gaping hole. Maybe I will be alright. But at the moment I don't want to go.

I know I'm processing, but this back and forth business is making me dizzy. I can feel that there are 2 distinct possibilities... fun and laughter vs. hurt and sadness. There isn't a clear front-runner at the moment.

Actually, there is... it's the hurt and sadness which is why I'm not ready to deal with Christmas and kids running around, and everyone else's laughter and I simply can't bear it.

So, mum, I'm not ready to get over it. I need some more time. I need to write some more. I need to process some more. I need some compassion, please!

In 2 weeks time it will probably be a different story but right now... NO!

Other people (my mum is one of those people) may be able to get over the grief of never having a baby in a heart beat, but obviously, I need a little extra time.

The idea of being around the children in my family breaks my heart. It seems I'm ok with my friends' children, maybe because they understand what I'm going through, but not the kids in my family. I've never allowed myself to get close to them. My husband does, but I keep them at arm's length. It hurts too much for me to know that I could have one just like that. These kids are a part of my gene pool, yet they aren't mine.

The kids in my family will never have cousins from my husband and me to know, to play with and to share the fun at family gatherings.

They will simply know me as Aunty who was there, but didn't ever have much to do with them. Sad really, yet I don't have the strength to open my heart wide enough. It hurts too much.

So please do not talk to me about Christmas. In fact, pretend that I'm not coming over and if I do then it's a bonus.

Aaaaaaaagggggggghhhhhhhhhhh!!!!!!!

Clarity Session

Setting boundaries is really important when you are healing.

Especially when others expect things from you that you are unable to give. You simply don't have the energy for it because you're using all your energy to heal.

Other people are going to be asking you to do things for them because they either don't know what you are going through or simply don't understand.

It is not their fault that they are asking and it is completely ok for them to ask, however, it is up to you to establish the boundaries of what is and is not appropriate for you.

A boundary is not an energetic wall or barrier preventing someone to get to you. It is a word that relates to building your inner strength muscle. It is like going to the gym to build your physical muscles.

Checking in with your inner knowing to make the choice to say yes or no to someone will help you create healthy boundaries.

As life continues while you are grieving, it is ok for you to say no. It is also ok for you to say yes and then change your mind.

Do what is right for you. Take care of yourself. Fill your energetic cup, and when it is overflowing, then you will have the ability to give to others.

This is a time in your life to be selfish and to be kind to yourself.

As you create healthy boundaries with others, you will find that you will heal faster and more completely. You will also have them established if you ever feel the need to take some time out in the future.

Most people will not understand what you are going through because they have either never gone through it themselves or because they are different people, their journey will not be the same as the one you are going through.

And that's ok too.

Chapter 14
A Couple of Days

I spoke with one of my wonderful girlfriends today.

She's having trouble with being exhausted as she has an 18-month-old and works a full-time job in 4 days. Something she never thought she would have to do as her little one was an unexpected bundle of joy.

She asked me how I was going, and I thought about it, and I felt fine. There were no underlying tears threatening me. There was no anything except feeling quite normal. I even felt good.

I had spent the past couple of days working on a course that I am going to bring out next week to help people get through the holiday season and all the loneliness and family issues that can arise. It's something I've been wanting to get organised for a while, but there has been a small mishap to derail me a little.

I also had a wonderful kinesiology session to balance my system. It's something I do with my clients, and it's good for me to have it done as well.

My friend asked me again how I was feeling. Digging a little deeper and I said, "In this moment, I feel fine. I don't know how I will feel in 2 hours or 2 days. I just know that right now, I'm good."

It was good to acknowledge that I was okay and this whole not having a baby was not going to encompass every waking moment.

I wish that I could say that I had moved through the process of grief, anger, and fear but it was not to be...

This afternoon I went shopping with my husband. Usually, he does the shopping for two reasons. Firstly, he enjoys it and secondly, I am not a fan. I really don't like going into shopping centres when my energy is low because as I found out today, the grief came back in full force.

Little babies, young kids, even kids throwing tantrums broke my heart. And then my husband started talking about us having children, and although the tears haven't started flowing, they are bubbling under the surface ready to be felt.

I wish I could run away. I wish we could move house. I wish we could go and live overseas so that I could get away from wanting to have children. But everywhere I go, that desire is still within me, and no amount of running away is going to make it disappear.

So after telling my husband that we don't need to put the house on the market, I've decided that I need to take some time every day to feel. 5 minutes, 10, 20 minutes. However long it takes to feel whatever I need to feel in that moment.

Even today when I was feeling fine, I didn't take the time to feel what I was feeling. I didn't open up my energy and feel the "fineness" and it was something that could have helped me move through this stage in my life.

The more I feel, the easier this becomes, and I know, as a practitioner, the quicker the ache of not having children will pass.

And so now I will feel...

Clarity Session

One of the most important parts of healing is our nutrition.

When we are grieving, our ability to regulate our food intake can be disrupted.

We can lose our appetite completely, or we can overeat.

Generally, eating the wrong sort of foods is what happens because the energy is focused on emotional healing.

When there is no strength to make good food choices, rely on your body to give you direction.

1. Take a deep breath and relax.

2. Ask your body to give you a yes response.

3. Ask your body to give you a no response.

4. Ask your body if it would be healing for you to eat (whatever meal is available to you at this moment).

5. Ask your body if it would be healing for you to drink some water in this moment.

6. Open your fridge and ask your body to show you what it would like to eat. Trust that you will receive a yes indication when you focus on a particular food item.

7. Be aware of the sad part of you wanting to eat what is not healthy for you. As you practice this process, you'll begin to notice the difference.

8. Eat what your body would like for happiness and health.

9. Avoid what your body would not like to eat, and you will find that your healing process becomes more in the flow of who you truly are.

As you practice this technique, you will find that you will be able to ask your body what it would like to eat for happiness and health and you will have an idea of exactly what it requires.

This process also allows you to create a deeper relationship with your body and your body shape may change and become healthier as a result of this connection.

Chapter 15
Baby Clothes

Over the past 6 years, I've collected a couple of things for my future baby.

And by a couple, I really mean 2 outfits. One for a baby girl and one for a baby boy. I also have a pregnancy diary that a friend bought me that I haven't unwrapped and a baby blanket that I bought while going through the last IVF treatment. It is so soft, and I have it wrapped around me at the moment.

All in all that's 4.

I think it's time to give the outfits away. They are sitting in the bottom drawer of my bedside table taking up emotional and physical space.

I know it's reactionary, but I just want to be done with it all. I understand that by giving things away when I have an emotional attachment could go either way. I could be free of the attachment to these imaginary children or I could... who knows what could happen!

My husband says to wait. I think he thinks that we still have a chance to fall pregnant naturally. Unless he knows something that I don't, I'm sure that ship has sailed.

Every time I think about giving the outfits away, I want to cry. It would be so final. Like I was giving my baby spirits permission to leave me.

Maybe this is something that I need to do.

I've been holding on so tightly to these babies that were going to be my children. I've been talking to them, asking them, pleading with them to come and join us in the physical. Oh so needy.

Why would anyone want to be the child of such a needy mother? I didn't realise I was being so emotionally dependent on children that aren't even here.

It's time to set them free. It's time for me to be free. It's time for someone else to get joy from these gorgeous little outfits. I'm keeping the blanket, and I can't give away a gift... what if I need it in the future!

Obviously, I still have my little toe in the "I still might get pregnant camp"!

I've just heard too many stories of when women give up trying, or they have their last round of IVF and as if by magic, they are pregnant. It's happened to a friend of mine. It's happened to friends of friends of mine and probably a number of other women I don't even know. And if it can happen to them, it can happen to me.

It's in the giving up and letting go. Releasing the energy of wanting so desperately that you will do almost anything for it.

The trick is that I can't give up in order to receive what I want. Unfortunately, it doesn't work that way. I need to get to the point where I have completely given up, and it would be a lot easier if my husband and other well-meaning friends didn't keep saying that it could still happen.

It's actually quite unkind for people to suggest that. I know that they want to stay positive but seriously, let it go! I'm going to, why can't you?

When is this roller coaster going to be over?! I really want to be done with it. It's so exhausting.

It's time to ask: Am I willing to allow this to be over?

Could I?

Would I?

When?

Now!

I'm ready to donate the gorgeous baby outfits today...

And maybe I won't.

Clarity Session

Giving up and letting go are the most difficult things to do.

We have been taught to focus on something, work at it and then it will come to fruition. However, this isn't always the case. Especially when things don't show up as planned.

However, letting go of how hard you are holding onto wanting to get pregnant can also be the opening for the flow to create that beautiful baby you wish for.

I know you would have been given this advice many times: "Just go on holiday, relax and focus on something else and you'll fall pregnant."

And it may just happen. However, when this is not happening for you, there may be a part of you that is not allowing yourself to let go.

Unfortunately, the process of letting go is not possible when you are trying to let go, because what happens is that you are trying to control the letting go process to get something out of letting go!

It's a catch 22, and if you have an inkling of control "freakiness" (that is a technical term) in you, this will relate to you.

Letting go is a combination of trusting that there is something more in store for you and being completely fed up with the situation.

These questions, when asked to your other than conscious mind can help you with the process of letting go.

1. "Could I let go of wanting to be pregnant?"

2. "Would I let go of wanting to be pregnant?"

3. When?

When you are able to honestly say yes to the first two questions, and now to the last, you are on your way to being completely free from the constraints that energetically prevent many from becoming pregnant.

When you are ready to go to the next level of letting go, these questions will assist in the process.

1. "Could I let go of everything that is attached and related to me wanting to get pregnant?"

2. "Would I let go of everything that is attached and related to me wanting to get pregnant?"

3. "When?"

Remember, when you can honestly say yes to the first two questions, and now to the third, you are ready for the final question.

1. "What else is possible in my life?"

Let go of looking for the answer as it will find you.

Chapter 16
One Song

There is a song by the band Train, and that is the only thing that can snap me out of feeling sad. Every other song I listen to is either blah or makes me cry. Whereas when I hear this song by Train, my heart immediately starts to dance and the happiness that is hiding within me shines through.

The song is "Save Me San Francisco" and even before the words are sung, the beat gets me going.

The lyrics then gets me singing, and after the song is over, I am feeling a whole lot better. It's always been a good song for me, although I would have thought that I had other favourite songs to get me through this time, yet this is the song of the moment.

I've been high, I've been low

I've been yes, and I've been oh hell no!

Luckily my husband has this song on most of our playlists as it has always been a favourite, but I think I need to be playing it around the clock to help me through my days.

I just played it, and I got goosebumps. I have no idea what it is about this song, but it is helping me through some emotional turbulence, and I am grateful.

So thank you Train for your music that resonates with me and allows the joy to shine again.

And now I will dance...

Clarity Session

You are constantly receiving communication.

Whether it is through sound, visions, feelings or all of them together.

And it is up to you to take notice and decipher what is being said.

The best way to find out the meanings of what is being communicated is to ask questions.

2. Take a deep breath and relax.

3. "Could I please have more clarity with what is being communicated to me?"

4. "What does (your specific piece of information) mean to me?"

    Does it remind you of someone or something?

    Do you get a feeling from it?

    Does it cause your body to move in a certain way?

1. If in doubt ask a trusted friend if the information you are receiving reminds them of something to do with you.

2. Remember that the best source of understanding comes from your inner knowing and not through other people's filters.

Don't worry if you find yourself analysing the information too much. Let it go and know that the answer will come to you when you are ready to hear it.

Chapter 17
I Wish

I JUST WISH I WAS PREGNANT. I REALLY DO.

I caught myself the other day googling false pregnancy tests, the hook effect and pregnant after period, just to find a sliver of hope that I could be pregnant.

I know I'm not, but I have a headache, really sore boobs and I'm weeing like there is no tomorrow. I just wish I was pregnant.

Once again, I know I'm not, and we're not going to be trying anymore but...

This is the first time that I am truly jealous of other women having children. While we had a chance, I was able to separate their life from mine, but I was watching a crappy reality show (you can tell I'm having a low day) and there was a woman having her first ultrasound and I saw and heard the baby's heartbeat. I think my heart broke all over again.

The pregnancy (on this show) was unexpected, and they kept saying "Everything happens for a reason." So what's my reason for not getting pregnant?

What's the lesson here that I'm not getting?

If I'm not supposed to have children, then why do I want them so badly?

And now that we've stopped trying, why can't I let it go?

I wish I had a family.

I woke up with my song ("Save me San Francisco") in my head, and I think it was a sign of the type of day I would be having.

Every time I feel my heart breaking I'm opening my heart up to more love from the universe. Opening, opening, opening so that the pain will dissipate into the ethers. Open some more and more...

I'll let you in on a little secret. I took a pregnancy test yesterday. Which is completely ridiculous as I'm on my 14th cycle day today! But I just had to check even though I knew what the answer was going to be.

I think I'm addicted to wanting to be pregnant. I can't let go of it. It is an old habit just hanging around that I no longer need.

This addiction no longer serves me as I have other things to occupy my life with and I'm ready to let it go.

This infertility no longer serves me, and I'm ready to let that go as well and whatever is attached to it, can leave too!

I still wish I was having a baby, but I'm not so I am going to pick myself up and get on with my day.

And the tears are hiding in the background...

Clarity Session

Sometimes it can look as though the grieving process is going backwards and that you'll never see the end of it.

However, it can simply be another aspect to it, another part of the journey.

Think back to a time 10 years ago when you were upset about something.

Is the situation still the same or have you moved on? Has time passed and are you living a different life now?

For most of us, I would say that yes, life is different than it was 10 years ago.

And in 10 years time, life will be different again.

One thing that is consistent in life is change, and that's why this grief will pass.

1. Take a deep breathe and relax.

2. Acknowledge to yourself what you are feeling.

3. Allow it to be ok to feel what you are feeling.

4. Know, that this too will pass.

5. And breathe.

Who knows the exact time and date, yet one day out of the blue, it will have passed.

We are doing really well in our journey. We're in this together, and we are ok.

Chapter 18
My Life on Hold

I can't believe what I have put off in my life because I wanted a family.

I've not applied for contracts just in case I was pregnant. I've adjusted my business so that I would be able to continue it and have a family. I've ended relationships because I wanted a family and they weren't ready.

I've made so many life choices because I wanted a family and now look at me!

Yes, I have a business where I can work from anywhere in the world, but I have so much spare time on my hands. I'm trying to figure out what I am going to do with all this time.

I've missed out on some great opportunities because I was hoping to be pregnant. I didn't want to start things in case I couldn't finish them.

I planned out my whole life only to have the universe give me something completely different.

If I had my time over, I would have let go of all expectations of what I would like my life to be and said yes to so much more.

I would probably have ended up in the same place anyway, so what does it matter how I got here?

I never used to believe in fate and having a pre-destined life path, but now, I'm not so sure.

All of the people who have goals and achieve them, who's to say that their life wasn't planned that way. And all the other people who have goals and don't achieve them didn't have their lives planned so that they would learn from not achieving!

Maybe before I came to this planet, I said, "I've had children in past lifetimes, and I'll probably have them in future lifetimes. How about I skip this lifetime. I learn the lesson of wanting something and not receiving it. Won't that be fun!"

What a fabulous life lesson and one I hope never to have to learn again!

Now that I am past baby making age (for me), Universe, what would you like me to do for the rest of my life? I'm all yours. All you have to do is show me the way, and I will follow because the way I do it doesn't work at all.

Who knows what will show up... or when...

Clarity Session

When you have a desire, sometimes everything else can fall by the wayside.

Friends and family who don't know what you are going through or don't understand are avoided.

Fertility appointments are made paramount, and other plans are put on hold.

Now it's time to surrender to the Universe.

Throw it all up in the air and say, "Here, you take it!"

Have you ever heard the saying, "Tell the Universe your plans and wait for it to laugh?"

Well, sometimes this is the case.

We think that something is the best direction for us, and on some level, it may be. However, sometimes magic can come from disaster.

Life hasn't worked out the way we would have liked, and now it's time to ask the question, "What's next?"

Every morning and every night ask your other than conscious mind questions like:

"What is the next step in my life?"

"Please show me the next step in my life?"

Remember not to look for the answers. Simply stay open to the possibilities that will show up in your life and go for it!

Chapter 19
Radical Hysterectomy

I WAS THINKING ABOUT WHY I HAVE A reproductive system. It obviously doesn't work so why do I even have it?

I do realise that my reproductive system does more for my body than grow humans, however, an appointment I made ages ago with my gynecologist came up the other day. The Fertility Specialist suggested I have a laparoscopy as I had a history of endometriosis 15 years ago. I have since been on herbs, and it seems to have cleared it up.

I was going to cancel it, but I thought, what the heck. I'll go and see what comes of it.

I'm sitting in the waiting room talking to my guides or whoever would listen to me asking them to give me a clear sign whether to have a laparoscopy, a lapendectomy (because the endometriosis was at the back of my uterus), a full hysterectomy or no surgery whatsoever.

The gynecologist was a locum. A very pleasant man who after looking at my medical history said that he would not do a laparoscopy or a lapendectomy but the only option was a radical hysterectomy and immediately go into menopause.

I knew I could get a second opinion, but this was the sign that I needed. As soon as he said this, my body clenched and I couldn't conceive of losing my body parts just because they weren't doing what I wanted.

It turns out that the doctor was well versed in herbal medicine, and when I said that I had cleared up endometriosis with the help of herbs, he suggested that if any of the symptoms returned to go straight back onto the herbs.

Why have full blown surgery when you can heal the issue with herbs?

I know that the gynecologist that is normally at this clinic would never have suggested this, so it seems that something was listening to me.

So the deal is that I am keeping my parts and if necessary, I will use herbs to clear up any imbalances that may or may not occur in the future.

On a side note, the thought of never even having the slightest possibility of having children was what freaked me out the most. It's so final. That would be it. Never! Ever!

I couldn't do it. I couldn't give up the chance of having children even if it may never happen.

I love my reproductive system even if it doesn't work properly.

Clarity Session

Listen to your inner knowing.

Just because a treatment works for one person, does not mean that it will work for everyone.

It would be easy if one size fits all, however, we all have slightly different genetic makeup which is why our treatments all need to be individualised.

Connect in with your inner knowing by breathing, being present and asking questions (without thinking about the answers) and take your time choosing what is right for you and your family.

Too many times when we are low on energy we give our power over to others. When we feel overwhelmed and don't know what to do, this is the most important time to connect with our inner knowing.

1. Breathe

2. Where are you? Inside your body? Outside your body? In a building? In a car?

3. Ask questions... ask for a sign, a movement, an indication for the next step in your journey.

You may not receive answers immediately, and the answers may come in a round about fashion, so take your time and know that you will receive the answers you are looking for.

Chapter 20
We Are Childless

We were walking the pups last night, and I had to remind myself that this is my life. This is who I'm with, this is where we live, and this is what I do.

There will be no little ones coming and disrupting our lives causing us to think of other things to do during the days and even getting us to move homes so that they will have space to play and grow.

This is it. My husband and I can travel as much as we want. We don't have to worry about school holidays and other kid agendas taking over.

We don't have to worry about school zones, after school activities, bullying, drugs or anything else. It's something that doesn't concern us directly.

It feels really weird because I have been setting up my life thinking that one day I will need to think about breastfeeding, baby wearing, home births, water births, hospital births, cesarian births, parenting styles and so much more.

I now have permission to put all of that down. It is no longer required for our life. The only thing is, we have a gaping hole in our lives. What are we going to do now?

What am I going to concern myself with?

Most of my close friends have children. What do I have in common with them? I have other friends who don't have children, but one of the reasons we moved house to be around the friends who have kids so that our children will be around our friend's children.

There is a gaping hole. I don't know what I am going to do with it.

What will I do? Who will I be?

Something that I thought I would never do, actually, that's not true. I thought I would do it when I had kids and that was gardening. I have been out in the garden lately. Not because I have to, just because it feels good.

That's a start...

What will I do? Who will I be now that I am childless...

Clarity Session

Put down the past to stay open to the future.

When your life changes trajectory, you may feel a little lost, and that's ok.

Take time in that lost feeling because what is actually happening is you are getting a pause. A rest, before the next chapter in your life begins.

Enjoy it! Relish it! Breath it in because this is the time where you are opening up for the possibilities to show up.

It's the time to give yourself over to self-care, meditation, massage, taking up a hobby and doing what gives you the most joy.

Ask questions to your other than conscious mind that allows you to open up to your life's purpose. For example:

"Universe, show me my purpose?"

"Universe, show me love?"

"What if I lived my life's purpose?"

"Universe, allow me to be open to your whispers and directions for the next step in my life?"

If you don't take that moment to pause, it is more difficult for the next step in your life to show itself to you. It will still show up, it may just take a little longer.

So, breathe and take a break from it all.

Know that the next step in your life is coming to you and you don't have to do a thing for it to arrive.

CHAPTER 21
I'M ALONE

I AM ALONE IN THE HOUSE WITH the pups and the cats of course, but I am alone. My husband has gone back to work after the Christmas/New Year break, and it is very quiet.

There are no sounds coming from the kitchen. There is no cricket on the TV. Apart from Max (pup) snuffling and outside noises, there is nothing.

I know I have work to do. I know that my life is ahead of me waiting for me to start, yet I feel like I'm in suspended animation. Not quite in my body, not quite out of it.

If the pups hadn't got me up for their breakfast this morning, I would probably still be in bed. I could probably stay in bed for a very long time. I simply don't have any energy. I thought about how sleeping in wouldn't be an option if I had children... oh well.

Over the past couple of weeks, I've been doing things with my family and husband that I probably could have done without. I think I needed a little more me time and my body is telling me all about it.

We're organising renovations on our house, we're fighting, and the balance of power is shifting back and forth between us. Our stuff is coming up and being shoved in our face because I started a program to help clients upgrade their relationships. This happens a lot. When I start to work on clients issues, underlying issues in my life start to come to the surface.

Do we want to stay together?

Do we want to take a break from each other?

Do we like each other?

It seems that one of the main reasons we are together is to have children and now that a family is no longer in the equation, what's holding us together?

Do we respect each other?

Do we care about each other?

Are we in limbo just putting one foot in front of the other?

Is this the person I would like to be with for the rest of my life?

In this moment, I don't know what I want. I know that I'm not going to be making any big decisions until I know the answers to these questions and more. I know that I am going to take things one day at a time and I know that this is a process I am going through, and I don't know where I'll end up.

I have a funny feeling that if I didn't have animals to look after, I would have moved to another country for a while away from life to take stock of what is going on inside me. I am unsettled. I am alone, and I don't know what is going to happen in my life.

And now he's gone back to work, and the house is quiet again.

I think I might take a nap...

Clarity Session

It's natural to re-evaluate your life while pausing.

Re-evaluate your relationship.

Re-evaluate your friends and family.

Re-evaluate every aspect of your life.

Remember this is the time to ask the big questions, to surrender and open up to what else is possible in your life.

Having a baby may not be one of those possibilities, not in this lifetime at least. However, we are so much more than being mothers and women have a beautiful feminine power that when opened up we can create so much more in this life.

Are you ready to the possibility of opening up and stepping into your power?

Asking questions such as:

"What is the next step in our relationship?"

"Show me what our relationship means to us?"

"Show me how I can contribute to my relationship?"

"What is one thing I can do today to contribute to my life?"

"What if my life turns out better than I could ever imagine?"

You can start with baby steps and then as you become stronger, you'll start asking questions that not only change your immediate world but others as well.

And then let the questions go...

Chapter 22
Waiting

It's day 28 of my cycle and my period is due at some stage.

This is the first cycle after the embryo transfer, and I don't know what is going to happen. My cycles are normally around the 33-day mark, but they can come anywhere from day 28 to 35.

My boobs are sore, and I'm bloated which have both been normal throughout this cycle, so I'm not assuming that these symptoms are premenstrual.

I have done a lot of energetic work on my reproductive system over the past couple of weeks, so I really don't know what to expect. Will I get cramps or will it be one of those periods where you forget you even have it? I love those. Will I get moody or not? Will my period be on time or late? Who knows!

It is possible that I am pregnant as we have had unprotected sex, but I'm not even going to go there.

I'm in no man's land or rather no woman's land. Not knowing, waiting and really not giving a shit whether it comes or not.

It's a freedom, not waiting and wanting to know if I am pregnant or not. I had forgotten how that feels. I know it happened in my life before because there have been months, years where I abstained from sex due to not having a partner, yet all these years trying to get pregnant has made me lose sight of the ease of not wondering.

I am not going to have children, so it's time for me to put it out of my mind.

Ideally, it would be wonderful for me to have regular cycles with balanced hormones for optimal health where pregnancy is not even on my radar. Wouldn't that be bliss!

Over 6 years of marriage I've calculated that I've had approximately 60 cycles of continuous wondering and a lot of stress. And what for? Sweet F* All!

Why do we do this to ourselves?

Why can't we be happy with the present moment? Happy with what we have in our lives? Happy without a child?

What is the urge that keeps us going? The urge to be a mother.

I know it would be an amazing experience. I know that it would expand my consciousness. I know that there would be ups and downs. I know that balancing work and children would be challenging. I know that I may or may not have to give up some things that I do now that I am childless.

I know and understand these things, and this is why I kept going for over 6 years, but enough is enough!

Maybe once I get my period, I'll get into a routine that would allow me to create a life that I have no concept of in this moment. I'll be able to create something that takes me out of the realms of motherhood and little ones and contribute in a way that would be completely different from the life I thought I would lead.

Maybe I'll know once my period comes...

Clarity Session

This is something that I was told during my 6 years of dancing with infertility.

When you are done with trying to conceive a baby, go on birth control.

You may wonder why you would need it, if you've never been able to conceive before, however, using a form of controlled fertility brings ease to your life.

It allows you to let go of wondering if you are pregnant and lets you focus on other aspects of your life.

I'm not suggesting any particular form. That is a choice for you and your body, although learning about your fertility cycle is a great way to start.

How do you know if it is time for you? Connect with your knowing and ask.

1. Take a deep breath and relax.

2. Ask your body to show you a yes.

3. Ask your body to show you a no.

4. Ask your body if it is beneficial to use (fill in the blank) for birth control.

5. Ask if there is another form of birth control that would be more beneficial to your relationship and your body?

6. If there is, ask for it to show up in your life with ease.

Are you ready for birth control? Yes? Or not just yet?

Chapter 23
My Husband Is Grieving

I noticed the other day that my beautiful husband was struggling a little.

He's the type of man who you just know would make an excellent father. Whenever there is a child or baby around, he just turns to mush.

He would never admit it though.

I looked at him last night, and he looked so sad it made me cry. The heartache that we are both going through for something that we said we could do without is enormous. I don't think I realised just how much it was affecting him.

He's been so busy looking after me. Wondering if I'm ok, that he hasn't had a chance to grieve.

I don't think that he is ready to give up as it took him a while to get on board with having children. He was 40 when we met and had given up on the idea that he was going to be a father, so switching that thought process back on took a couple of years, and it's probably going to take a couple of years to switch it off.

I am devastated that I am unable to give him children. He is loving and giving, and even though he would worry about our children constantly, we would balance each other out.

I wish he would open up to me and he will in time, just not yet.

He is coping in his own way.

And allowing him to grieve in his own way is all I can do...

Clarity Session

Grief can bring people together, and it can pull them apart.

Some like to grieve together and others alone.

For the ones who choose to grieve alone, all we can do is be there for them if they ever need us.

We are unable to go through the grieving process for another as everyone has their own journey and we all grieve differently.

Suggestions to ease the pain may or may not be welcome depending on the stage of grieving.

Just remember how it feels when others tell you how or what you should be doing to get over your heartache.

Be aware of what your partner is going through and if they are open, communicate that they are not alone.

Most of the time it is enough to walk next to your partner as they process the loss of their family dreams.

A process that may help is the love bubble technique.

1. Take a deep breath and relax.

2. Imagine your partner in front of you.

3. Imagine enveloping them in a bubble of love.

4. This bubble expands out into the universe allowing the love to grow.

5. Know that you are also in a bubble of love and as that grows your love expands as well.

6. Trust that the bubbles will heal all that is there to be healed and you will be loved beyond measure.

Ask yourself, "What's one thing that I could do to contribute to the happiness of my partner's life today?"

And go and do it.

Chapter 24
So They Say

We had some friends over on New Year's Eve which was really great. We loved having them here, and they enjoyed it too.

As I was going to get a glass of water, one of my friends asked if I was pregnant.

My response was, "No, I'm just fat!" because my stomach is bloated.

I thought it was hilarious, she was embarrassed, and we all had a laugh.

The main reason why she asked was she still thinks I'm going to have children and me not having a glass of champagne was a sign that I may be pregnant.

My friends are all very intuitive. They know when people are going to be pregnant, when relationships aren't great and so much more. I'm surrounded by psychics and mediums, and we can't get away with anything!

My friends are still keeping baby clothes for me. They just know!

Unfortunately, these baby clothes will not be needed as they don't fit my dogs or cats and even if they did, I wouldn't be making my animals wear them!

I'll let my beautiful friends keep thinking whatever they desire and I'll give them a couple of years before I tell them to send their baby clothes to someone who is actually pregnant.

Because there is still a glimmer of hope that they could be right, that I could still have a baby, that is allowing for those couple of years before the clothes get redistributed.

Yet I cannot allow myself to live in fantasy land. I would end up in the looney bin or worse if I didn't put a stop to it. They can have all the dreams they want for me, I just can't do it. The tears would fall. I would never get out of bed, and my life would be wasted. All for a dream that wouldn't come true.

No babies for me... so I say...

Babies are coming for me... so they say...

Clarity Session

Laughter is the best medicine.

Sometimes it doesn't feel that way, and if someone had told me to laugh when I first started to write this book I would have wanted to be violent towards them!

So how about we pretend.

Go and look into a mirror (because looking at yourself doing this will crack you up!)

Say out loud...

Ha ha ha, he he he

Ha ha ha, he he he

Ho ho ho, he he he

Ho ho ho, he he he

Ha ha ha, he he he

And keep going until you find the whole process so ridiculous you start to giggle naturally.

Are you ready to make this a daily practice?

Chapter 25
Exhaustion

I AM SO TIRED THAT I'M REALLY not doing much at the moment.

It's cycle day 34, and there is no sign of my period.

I keep having to remind myself that it is under five weeks ago that I found out that we weren't going to have children. I obviously expect myself to be fine with everything now when clearly it is not. My life is supposed to fall into place, and my energy levels are supposed to reflect that.

Well, let me tell you, it ain't happening that way.

Today is one of the few days that I have been able to get out of bed without feeling like my head is going to explode and that I will actually be doing something fulfilling. I had no idea what may be fulfilling today, but I was willing to find out.

Yesterday, I got into the garden and weeded my heart out. This is something that is almost unheard of, yet I've been finding that there is something healing about the earth and connecting with it that is shifting my energy levels.

I also decided yesterday that my body needed a little extra help. I'm going to start taking a supplement solution three times a day to get some nutrients into my beautiful body.

And today I am drinking it.

I'm still tired today, so we'll see how I go throughout the week.

When my energy levels are this low there are a couple of things I need to do for myself:

1. Find out if the energy leak is spiritual, emotional, physical or something else.

2. Ask for help from various sources – someone in the physical or energetic realm.

3. Administer what is required to heal the energy leak.

So, I've muscle tested that it's an emotional leak. That's not really a surprise, and the help that will heal the leak will come from the energetic realm.

However, because the feelings are more physical than emotional, I'm going support myself with the supplement and good food.

I've found some software that I've been guided to use on a regular basis to help heal the energetic leak and oh my god, I hope it works because I feel like I could sleep for a million years!

I've done the process that the software suggests and this is the first time in 5 weeks that I haven't been craving chocolate. Usually, by this time of the day I'm eating a mountain of it and I can't stop. I have to fill my bucket of energy as it seeps out of the hole in the bottom somehow and chocolate seems to be my way.

I'll let you know how I go as I keep on healing my beautiful, emotional energy leak...

Clarity Session

When focused on emotional healing, having the energy to look after yourself physically can be too overwhelming.

As you start to heal, look at what you are eating.

Are you getting the nourishment you need?

Your body has been put through the wringer with your infertility journey, and grieving just adds to that.

Go and get yourself checked out by your health care professional.

How are your vitamin and mineral levels?

Do you need iron, iodine, b vitamins, or something else?

Now that you know how to tune into your body, ask it.

And if you can't get a clear answer from your body, ask it to guide you to a health care practitioner who can give you the clarity so you can support your body to support you.

It could also be that you have an energetic leakage in your field.

If this is the case, most times you can simply ask your other than conscious mind to heal it or guide you to someone who can.

Chapter 26
Keep On Trying

We went to a friend's house for dinner the other night, and she has a beautiful 18-month little girl.

I have known this little girl prior to her conception, and it seems she remembers me too. I've only seen her a handful of times since she's been born, but she was quite happy to sit on my lap and give me lots of cuddles and share her crackers with me, which the parents say is very unusual.

I remember saying to my friend to be careful if she didn't want to be pregnant because there is baby energy around her. She didn't pay much attention because she was in her early 40s and hadn't been able to get pregnant yet.

I was the 1st to know that she was pregnant and I went to an ultrasound when the father couldn't make it.

All while trying to get pregnant myself and it wasn't hard in the slightest.

The main reason I was able to support my friend was because it wasn't about me. In fact, her pregnancy had nothing to do with me. It was all about her, and that was the way it should be.

When I focused on her and her bub, it was easy. If I ever turned it around on me, which I rarely did, it was hard.

I say, go for the easy any day.

This little girl was unplanned on the conscious level. On the soul level, it was definitely a plan and one that worked out beautifully.

What if our conscious wishes could match our subconscious wishes. I think if that was the case, we would be more careful of what we wished for and it would also save a lot of heartache. However, we wouldn't get all the wonderful surprises that we don't think of because we are limited by our imagination.

What if...?

The next day, my husband and I were having a chat. This is a chat that we have been having for the last 6 years.

"Do you want to keep trying?"

He says yes, but doesn't want to stop drinking, change his eating habits or do anything else that may help in the conception of a child. He's decided that if we live like he wants the child will just show up, like a teenage pregnancy!

I don't have the energy, and the more I see him doing things that prevent his sperm being at optimal levels, it breaks my heart even more.

I still want to have a child, I just don't want to go through the pain of not getting pregnant again.

I think I can be happy living vicariously through my friend's children. We have nieces and nephews, some are adults, and the rest are teenagers who we are in our lives. The majority of our friends have children, so it's not as if we won't have them in our lives and that means that we can still go travelling whenever we want.

As if that is compensation for not having children.

So I've left it up to him. If he wants children he can continue to want them, and we'll continue to have unprotected sex, so you just never know.

But I can't, I simply can't. It just hurts too much...

Clarity Session

Do what is best for you.

Unless you are working as a team, supporting each other and connecting intimately, you will not have the energy to carry your partner through the conception process.

Getting pregnant is a team effort.

Relationships are a great way to see what is going on within you.

Is there an aspect of you that is not willing to join the team?

Is there an area in your life where you aren't willing to give pregnancy your all?

Take a look at your partner and ask yourself "Where in my life am I like them?"

It may not be obvious. It may not even be in this lifetime, yet if you are willing to heal that part of you that is reflected in them, you may find a change in the relationship.

1. Take a deep breath and relax.

2. Ask yourself, "Everywhere I have aligned and agreed and resisted and reacted to [your partner's behaviour], am I willing to let it go?"

3. Could I? Yes?

4. Would I? Yes?

5. When? Now?

And then let it go...

Chapter 27
Asking Questions

Have you ever been in the situation where you are asking God, the Universe, whoever will listen, "What is going on with my life?" or even, "What am I supposed to do now?"

I'm sure everyone has at some stage in their life.

Well, I'm at that stage now. I'm in total bewilderment. I had an idea of what I was doing, what was going to happen in life and now, who knows?

I'm not really expecting answers because I'll only come up with things that I think I know, not answers that will give me the truth of what my life is. What I am.

Yes, I am going deep.

I've been at this type of crossroads many times in my life, and many times it's just before I move interstate or even overseas. Yet this is different. I am stronger within myself, and I know myself better, so I am more conscious of what the consequences would be.

For example, last week I was certain my husband and I were going to part ways. Absolutely ready to grab the dogs and leave. (He gets custody of the cats). Yet I knew it was the grief talking and it was important for my personal development to stay put.

This week we are better. There is still much to process, but we are better.

I'm also more aware of my thoughts.

Last week my niece was looking for a ride to a town about two hours from where we live, and I thought that a drive might be nice, and then I let it go.

I now know that when those random thoughts pop into my mind, and then I wait and see, I generally get the chance to fulfil them.

I am currently writing this from a wonderful cafe in that town two hours from where we live waiting for my niece and her girlfriend to finish their photo shoot, and it's been so much fun.

Although it may not seem like it, this little road trip was an answer to the questions I have been asking.

This is what I am doing in my life. I am being of service. I am being where I need to be. I am being productive, and I am healing.

I am being kind to others, smiling, laughing and appreciating the little things.

I am taking life one day at a time. I am being gentle on myself, and I am opening my heart.

I have been humming and ha'ing about hiring a cleaner for our home. I'm not the best at keeping on top of cleaning the house, and I have other things I enjoy.

As I was mopping the other day, I was opening myself up to the Universe and wondering what was next. A text from a friend came through recommending a cleaner, and now I have one coming once every 4 weeks to start with.

One step at a time my life will come together. I don't know where I will end up. I don't know what I will do between now and the end, and I'm ok with that...

Clarity Session

Be prepared to go with the flow...

Life is a journey full of experiences, and it's up to you to be willing to say yes to them.

Sometimes they creep up on you and other times they are shoved in your face.

How you respond to them is how much fun the experiences or adventures will be.

Resistance is also an emotion that you can dive into and come out the other side, and when treated as such it is easier to stay open to your life.

1. Take a deep breath and relax.

2. Acknowledge your resistance.

3. Remember that the Universe will never give you anything that you can't handle.

4. Say to yourself, "BRING IT ON!"

5. Dive into the resistance.

6. Feel yourself flying through it can coming out the other side.

7. Create your life from the other side of resistance.

Are you resisting life? Or are you ready to flow?

Chapter 28
Divorce

The other day, my husband and I almost split up.

It's something that I never thought would happen to us, yet we were so close to it, it was unbelievable.

We went through 24 hours of tears, heartache, and revelations.

My husband told me that he didn't find me attractive and this is something that we both know isn't true, and yet, sometimes it comes up. Most of the time, I bury it underneath day to day life.

This is not my stuff, this is his journey.

However, after 6 years+ of dealing with it and coming to the realisation that I don't need him as a sperm donor (harsh I know), I could possibly be with a man who thought I was the beez kneez!

I didn't have to put up with his issues. Because we all have plenty. And I was ready to go.

And for the first time, he was ready to let me go.

Which of course meant that I could go.

Throughout all the soul searching and tears (and there were tears, heartwrenching ones) there was a turning point as we were driving to go out to dinner with friends.

He turned to me and said, "So this is it. It's over."

And I could easily have said yes. However, I said, "I don't want it to be."

It was something that came from my soul, not from the level of the heartache and grief of not having a child but knowing that we are soul mates and even with all our idiosyncrasies we love each other dearly.

My husband realises that the lack of sexual attractiveness has nothing to do with me. He is attracted to me. I've seen it and I know deep down he knows it too, but there's something else going on. And I don't know how to help him.

The next morning something had shifted. We were a little battered and bruised yet we knew that we were going to make it.

And he has told me that he's going to take a look at what's really going on... Hoorah!!!!

So we shall see how it goes.

We thought that we were ready to break up, yet it seems as though an upgrading was occurring.

We all get to the stage where we can act on the level of the personality or from the level of the soul and this crossroads we chose the soul. Who knows if we will stay together until death do us part. We will have to make a choice every time we need to and who knows what we will choose.

I'm glad we have chosen to stay together this time.

Clarity Session

Is this the point for you to go your separate ways or is this the next step in your relationship?

When we come to a crisis in our relationships, many believe that leaving is the best option. And if you are under extreme emotional or physical abuse I would agree with that. However, if you could completely let go of the past, all the blame, resentment and forgiveness, would you choose to be in a relationship with your partner.

If the answer is, "I don't know," then it may be time to consult your inner knowing.

1. Take a deep breath and relax.

2. Ask, "If I lived in the highest expression of who I really am, would I continue with this relationship or would I leave?"

3. What if you couldn't make a wrong choice?

4. What if you couldn't go in the wrong direction?

Remember, your other than conscious self has all the answers for you, and when it is time to leave, you will know without any doubt.

You will know.

And then it is time to leave and create a new relationship with the same partner or someone else.

Chapter 29
But...

The other day, I learned how to cleanse my house of energies that did not support us. I learned how to connect and work with the property's guidance, and then I did it on our property.

Within minutes, the depression that had been creeping up on me over the past couple of months lifted. It was amazing. Incredible even!

Our property's guides are named Create and Joy, and they are here to serve the property and its tenants. I am so pleased I have met them because, from the moment I did, I felt so completely different.

My yearning for children has almost gone. It doesn't mean that if a couple of kids didn't show up that I wouldn't be ecstatic, however, it's not ruling my life any more.

I have energy.

I have creativity.

I have joy.

I am opening up to new opportunities.

But... I feel guilty that I am ok. Weird I know!

It's like I should be sad that I don't have a baby. I should be grieving for the end of my dreams. I should be unhappy... just because it should take longer to process all these feelings.

But no, I don't feel sad. I'm almost at the stage where I am excited about life. In fact, I am excited about life!

I have lived in over 25 houses/apartments throughout my life, and I have felt the difference in energies, and when we moved into this house, we were happy, however, with all the disappointment of not conceiving a child and whatever is going on with my husband, it brought out the sadness in the property that we didn't connect with initially.

Once we had connected to it, it just kept growing and growing until depression was ready to engulf me.

Now the connection has been broken and cleared out of the property, who knows what will show up in our life?

Clarity Session

Connecting with your property guides is as easy as taking a breath and asking a question...

1. Take a deep breath and relax.
2. Ask, "What is required for me to connect with my property guides?"
3. You may feel something, you may have a vision, or you may hear something or nothing at all.
4. And breathe
5. Ask, "What is required to assist with the healing of the property guides?"

There are generally two of them, and they encompass the sky above and the ground below your property.

The guides are there to support you, so ask them what they need to do this for you.

If the guides are not happy or they need something from you, ask your other than conscious mind to assist with that.

Trust that your other than conscious mind will take care of it for you or guide you to someone who will.

Chapter 30
Heartbreaking

We are currently renovating our bathrooms and to prepare, I needed to clean out our ensuite.

So I'm cleaning and moving lotions and potions from the ensuite to the main bathroom or into a box or the bin, and I come across some leftovers from the last fertility process.

I haven't thought about babies and everything that goes along with it for what seems like a while to me, although it is probably only a week and as soon as I see what's in the baby making bag, I'm all teary again!

If I had let myself, and I probably should have, I would have curled up in a ball and wept in the way that it feels like your heart is being wrenched from your body. If I had done that, I would be writing this feeling like I had processed it and can move on.

However, I didn't weep. I suppressed it and continued preparing the bathroom, and now I feel like curling up in a ball all sad and sorry for myself because I don't have a baby.

Things that you think you have dealt with are the issues that come and bite you in the arse when you least expect it to. They have a way of blindsiding you and keep niggling at you until they are resolved.

Just as I thought I had pushed it down enough so I wouldn't ever have to deal with it again, when we went out later that night, a friend of mine was talking about how relieved he was that a pregnancy scare turned out to be just that, a scare. He went on and on about the fact that he didn't have to worry about kids and that he was so lucky to be out of that situation!

I understand that it is his choice not to have children, yet life has a way of shoving contradictory choices in your face when you don't want to deal with them.

So here I am with the drilling and gutting of the ensuite going on in the background feeling like I've been hit by a brick because I wish I had a baby(ies).

I'm going to trust that this will process in its own time. I'm not going to force it. I'm going let my higher-self do its job and support me through it because I don't have the energy to do it on my own.

I've been through a rollercoaster of trying to become pregnant, and I don't know what to do anymore.

I'm giving up.

I'm done.

I'm tired of it all, and it's coming back to kick me in the guts when I least expect it.

Higher self, could you please download any lessons I require with regards to not getting pregnant and having children and resolve it on my behalf?

Thank you.

Clarity Session

And the journey continues...

Spring cleaning (even if it's not spring) is a wonderful way to remove old thought processes.

When you are grieving, you are energetically shedding the pain, the hurt, and the anger.

It is very important to make sure your pillow and mattress on your bed, couch or anywhere else you have been comforting yourself are cleansed, with a spray of essential oils or flower essences, candles or sage.

Thoughts and emotions are like dead skin. They accumulate in corners of the house and need to be vacuumed on a regular basis.

If you don't have these products on hand, there is a process that you can do to kick start the cleanse.

1. Take a deep breath and relax.

2. Imagine your house and the land where it resides.

3. Imagine standing at the front of your property.

4. Imagine a blue light flowing from the front of the property through every part of your property and home.

5. Trust that it will keep cleansing your property and home until it is fully cleansed energetically.

Also, remember that it is great to get your body moving and clean physically clean your house. Especially the pillows and bedsheets.

Chapter 31
A Pregnant Friend

It's been a while since my last chapter, and I've been busy living life.

I still have the baby blanket, that's not going away anytime soon. I know giving that up is something that can not be forced.

I've been creating a relationship course and needed a wingman to test some theories I was going to use as techniques in the course. So, of course, I called up an amazing friend of mine who used to be a little more connected to the going out scene than I am.

I hadn't seen her for a while and didn't realise how serious her relationship was.

And the first thing she said to me was "I'm pregnant."

I have always been happy for my friends who were pregnant. I've even been to ultrasounds with them when the dads couldn't make it! I've never had an issue with it at all, but this one hit me for six!

I'm not upset because she is pregnant. I'm not even upset because I'm not. I simply feel upset and I can't put my finger on why.

I didn't tell her I was upset because I needed to process my feelings. I'm not about to dump my issues on my beautiful friend who is glowing with pregnancy hormones.

What am I going to do? I feel like all the healing I have done has gone to waste, and I'm back at square one.

It may seem funny, but I wish I saw her more often. Even though we are very close, we only keep in touch sporadically. If I was more involved and connected with the pregnancy, maybe I would feel better because it would feel more like hers rather than a baby that I lost.

Who knows?

I know I haven't gone backwards, this is simply more healing that is required.

What I have since realised is that the trigger for some reason or other, was that in the womb, I didn't feel safe and my friend's pregnancy brought that up for me.

I simply have to remember that her pregnancy has nothing to do with my lack of pregnancy as I have done in every other instance.

So, how do I heal this heartache once and for all?

I would love to have children in my life. Adoption or fostering, for various reasons aren't viable for us.

I think it's time to call in for help.

I'm going to ask my higher self/other than conscious mind to heal this and everything related to it on my behalf.

Please also flood the area of my consciousness with love so this, whatever this is, is completed completely.

As I'm writing this, I can feel a weight lifting off me. The sadness is easing, and there is a shadow of a smile coming onto my face.

Life is full of opportunities, and I have so much to do in my life. All I need to do is, say yes.

I say yes to life!

Clarity session

Thanking the person or people who trigger your residual emotions is a great kindness as they are giving you something you were not able to give yourself.

At this point in the grieving journey, you've dived into the emotions, you've looked after yourself both physically and emotionally, you've made choices with your relationships, and you're more present every day.

It's now time to completely give this journey up.

You've experienced it, you've learned the lesson, and it's time for it to pass.

When you are ready...

Ask you higher consciousness, "Please heal this on my behalf if this is no longer serving me. If this is serving me in some manner, please show me what that is so that it can be healed gently and easily. Thank you."

See if you notice anything... a feeling, an emotion.

If not, go about your day, knowing that your other than conscious mind is doing the work for you on your behalf.

You are being supported.

Chapter 32
Opening to new possibilities.

What a journey! At the end of the last chapter, I felt like my process has been completed and I knew that what I had written needed to be published.

There are so many women who have support during the time when we are trying to conceive, yet when they make the choice to stop, we are left hanging.

This is one of the most important stages of a woman's life, where she needs more support than ever to be able to heal from the heartbreak and open up to a new and fulfilling life.

After a cathartic healing process miracles can occur. They have for me and will do for you too.

I am more fulfilled than I have been in years. My business is thriving and my husband and I are more connected than we have been for a while.

My body has changed, and I am having regular 28/29 day cycles for the first time in decades... and with very little pain.

There are 31 processes in this book that took me almost four months to complete, and I'm feeling great.

My intention for you, with the help of this book, is to heal from what is a truly heartbreaking time in our lives and create a life beyond your imagination.

Connect in with your inner knowing, re-establish a deeper love for yourself, your body and your partner. Keep asking the questions and staying open to the possibilities that will show up in your life.

As you practice and become aware of what your inner knowing is saying to you, your days will flow with miracles and your heart will be full of joy once again.

I wish you all the best in your life after the roller coaster that is the infertility journey. I see you, I know you, and you are beautiful!

About The Author

Rosemary de Vos lives in Perth, Western Australia

After suffering from anxiety and depression since she was a teenager, she found relief in Mind Body Medicine and Holistic Counselling which she started to study and practice in the early 2000s.

She loves to travel, explore different cultures and ask the deeper questions in life.

As an Intuitive Counsellor, she now facilitates ease and joy into every aspect of a person's life.

The question she asks herself and invites others to ask is;

"What can I be today to contribute to my life and the lives of others?"

You can find out more about Rosemary at her website: www.rosemarydevos.com

To receive your free gift:
http://rosemarydevos.com/bfn-gift

www.ingramcontent.com/pod-product-compliance
Lightning Source LLC
Chambersburg PA
CBHW031419290426
44110CB00011B/451